W9-BFC-014

DATE			

San Francisco

San Francisco

A Downtown America Book

Patricia Haddock

Dillon Press
New York

Collier Macmillan Canada
Toronto

Maxwell Macmillan International Publishing Group
New York   Oxford   Singapore   Sydney

Library of Congress Cataloging-in-Publication Data

Haddock, Patricia.
San Francisco / by Patricia Haddock.
(A Downtown America book)
Includes index.
Summary: Describes the past and present, neighborhoods, attractions, and festivals of San Francisco.
1. San Francisco (Calif.)—Juvenile literature. [1. San Francisco (Calif.)] I. Title. II. Series.
F869.S357H33 1988   979.4'61   88-20200
ISBN 0-87518-383-2

Macmillan Publishing Company, 866 Third Avenue
New York, NY 10022

Printed in the United States of America
  2 3 4 5 6 7 8 9 10

Photographic Acknowledgments

Photographs are reproduced through the courtesy of the California Office of Tourism (Tom Myers, Norman Prince); Exploratorium (Esther Kutnick); Ghirardelli Square; Patricia Haddock; © 1988 Malcolm F. Kimberlin (pages 12, 17, 22, 34, 38); © 1987 Susan Middleton (pages 32, 45); Mission Dolores; San Francisco Convention and Visitor's Bureau (Mark Gibson, Vano Photography); San Francisco Zoo (Susan Gilbert); Steve Elmore/Tom Stack & Associates; and U.S. Department of the Interior, National Park Service (Richard Frear). Cover: San Francisco Public Utilities Commission Photographic Department (William Owyang). A special thanks to S. Wilde and M. Kimberlin for their help with photographs.

Contents

Fast Facts about San Francisco

San Francisco: The City That Knows How; The City by the Golden Gate; The City of the Golden Hills; The City by the Bay; The City

Location: California coast, mid-state, northern tip of a peninsula bounded by the Pacific Ocean on the west, the Golden Gate on the north, San Francisco Bay on the east, and San Mateo County on the south

Area: City, 129 square miles (334 square kilometers), including several islands and a large area covered by water; consolidated metropolitan area, 7,960 square miles (20,616 square kilometers)

Population (1986 estimate*): City, 749,000; consolidated metropolitan area, 5,877,800

Major Population Groups: Whites, Asians, Hispanics, blacks

Altitude: Highest—Mount Davidson, 933.6 feet (285 meters); lowest—sea level

Climate: Average temperature is 50°F (10°C) in January, 59°F (15°C) in July; average annual precipitation, including rain and fog, is 22 inches (56 centimeters); average annual sunshine is 65 hours out of every possible 100 hours; city is known for its fogs; climate varies from neighborhood to neighborhood

Founding Date: 1776, chartered as a city in 1850

City Flag: Phoenix rising from flames

City Seal: Shield showing a ship entering the Golden Gate, supported by a miner to the left and a sailor to the right. Symbols of commerce, navigation, and mining lie at their feet. A phoenix rising from flames is above the shield; the city motto is below it—*Oro en Paz, Fierro en Guerra* ("Gold in Peace, Iron in War")

Form of Government: The city and county share the same boundaries and are governed by a mayor and a board of supervisors.

Important Industries: Tourism, finance, banking, retail

*U.S. Bureau of the Census 1988 population estimates available in fall 1989; official 1990 census figures available in 1991-92.

Festivals and Parades

February: Chinese New Year

March: St. Patrick's Day

April: Cherry Blossom Festival, Nihonmachi

May: Historic Trolley Festival (through October)

June: Cable Car Festival; Gay-Lesbian Freedom Parade

August: San Francisco County Fair

September: San Francisco Blues Festival Italian Festival

October: Blessing of Fishing Fleet; Columbus Day; Fleet Week; Grand National Rodeo, Horse Show and Livestock Exposition

November: Harvest Festival

December: Christmas Tree Lighting, Union Square

For further information about festivals and parades, see agencies listed on page 56.

San Francisco

BERKELEY

GOLDEN GATE STRAIT

ALCATRAZ ISLAND

GOLDEN GATE BRIDGE

TREASURE ISLAND

SAN FRANCISCO–OAKLAND BAY BRIDGE

PACIFIC OCEAN

OAKLAND

E MARINA

D TELEGRAPH HILL

PRESIDIO
GOLDEN GATE NATIONAL RECREATION AREA

RUSSIAN HILL

NORTH BEACH

EMBARCADERO

SAN FRANCISCO–OAKLAND BAY BRIDGE

PACIFIC HEIGHTS

SEA CLIFF

A

NOB HILL

CHINATOWN

SAN FRANCISCO BAY

NIHONMACHI

SOUTH OF MARKET

GOLDEN GATE PARK

G
F

EUREKA VALLEY

MISSION DISTRICT

CASTRO

N

NOE VALLEY

C

ST. FRANCIS WOOD

| miles | 0 | 1 | 2 | 3 | 4 |
| kilometers | 0 1 | 2 | 3 4 | 5 | 6 |

B

Points of Interest

A Transamerica Pyramid
B Candlestick Park
C San Francisco Zoo
D Fisherman's Wharf
E Palace of Fine Arts (Exploratorium)
F California Academy of Sciences
G M. H. de Young Memorial Museum

1

San Francisco— Here We Come

It has been called *The City That Knows How, The City by the Golden Gate, The City of the Golden Hills*, and *The City by the Bay*. It is San Francisco, and no one who lives here ever calls it *Frisco*.

San Francisco lies at the tip of a peninsula midway up the coast of California. Water surrounds it on three sides—the Pacific Ocean to the west, the narrow Golden Gate strait to the north, and San Francisco Bay to the east. San Mateo County meets the city at its southern border. The famous Golden Gate Bridge spans the strait between San Francisco and Marin County to the north. To the east, the San Francisco-Oakland Bay Bridge links the city to the city of Oakland across the bay. Several islands in San Francisco Bay and the Pacific Ocean are also part of the city, including Treasure Island and Yerba Buena.

A view across San Francisco, with the downtown area and San Francisco Bay in the background.

Fog often keeps San Francisco temperatures cool, especially in the summer.

In the Bay Area, ocean fogs keep the climate cool and comfortable year round. The foggiest months occur during the summer when California's inland valleys heat up and "pull in" the fog at the coast. When the valleys cool down in the fall, the coast heats up, and San Franciscans enjoy the warm, sunny days of September and October.

Even though San Francisco covers an area smaller than most other large cities, more than forty hills rise within its borders. Because its land area is so limited, the city has built upward. The financial district, Embarcadero, and South of Market district have the city's tallest buildings, including the fifty-two-story Bank of America world headquarters and the Transamerica Pyramid. These buildings hold some of San Francisco's most well known companies.

While tourism is San Francisco's largest business today, the city has been a banking and financial capital since the California gold rush days. Bank of America, founded in San Francisco, pioneered branch banks. Today, just about every major bank in the world has an office in San Francisco. Montgomery Street has been nicknamed the "Wall Street of the West" because its large banks and investment

The Transamerica Pyramid is one of San Francisco's tallest and best-known modern buildings.

firms look much like those of New York City's financial district.

Retailing is another big business in this bayside city. More than 10,000 retail stores range in size from small, local, one-of-a-kind shops to large national stores. Downtown San Francisco, centered around Union Square in the city's northeastern corner, forms the city's major shopping area. Union Square has many fashionable shops and big department stores. Other shops fill two unusual shopping centers that reflect the city's history. In earlier times, Ghirardelli Square was a chocolate factory, and the Cannery was a food-processing plant.

Unusual shopping centers and stores are one part of San Francisco's amazing variety. This is a city like no other, a city that offers something for everyone.

In San Francisco, one-hundred-year-old cable cars clank past modern high-rise office buildings. Early San Franciscans said the cable cars would not last.

The city created a park experts said could not be built. Then it constructed a bridge experts said could not be built. The park and the bridge are now two of the city's most famous landmarks.

The opening nights of the opera and symphony are major social events. Yet San Franciscans are just as proud of local rock groups like Huey Lewis and the News.

World leaders signed the United Nations Charter in San Francisco.

Ghirardelli Square at night.

The San Francisco 49ers and Giants play at Candlestick Park.

Beatniks, hippies, and rock and roll also had their beginnings here.

Gold miners and pioneers once made the city a "rough-and-ready" place to live. Today, San Francisco is a performing arts center, and attracts artists from around the world.

A cable car climbs a hilly street in downtown San Francisco.

There is never nothing to do in San Francisco. Sports fans can cheer the baseball Giants and football 49ers at Candlestick Park, fish the waters of the Pacific Ocean, and run the tough Bay to Breakers foot race. Local people and visitors enjoy going to well-known places such as Golden Gate Park and Fisherman's Wharf.

Even a walk down a city street offers the chance to see and do something different. On street corners, actors called mimes use their bodies and faces to act out wordless stories. A one-person band entertains shoppers in front of an elegant fashion shop. Flowers of every color and scent spill across concrete sidewalks at street corner flower stands. Musicians and singers perform jazz, rock, opera, country, and rhythm and blues music on street corners and in parks. Business people eat lunch while watching young skateboarders practice their skills in open-air plazas.

Throughout the year, city residents take part in festivals that reflect their international heritage. Chinese New Year in February, Japanese Cherry Blossom Festival in April, and Columbus Festival in October—these are just a few of the lively events that San Franciscans celebrate every year.

Today, people who come from China, Japan, Vietnam, the Philippines, India, Italy, Germany, France, Ireland, Spain, Mexico, Nicaragua, Peru, and many more countries call San Francisco home. The city has a Japanese neighborhood called Nihonmachi. The largest Chinese community outside Asia lives in the twenty-four blocks of Chinatown and spills over into the Italian neighborhood of North Beach. A large Hispanic neighborhood stretches east and south from the old Mission, the site where the city

A San Franciscan shops at a fruit stand in Chinatown.

Elegant, century-old homes line a San Francisco street not far from the glittering lights of downtown.

was first settled. Many other neighborhoods have large numbers of immigrants, or descendants of immigrants, from around the world.

San Francisco wasn't always a modern city with an international population. It started as a sleepy mission outpost of the Spanish in California. Later, in the mid-1800s, gold was discovered in the foothills of the Sierra Nevada mountains. As thousands of gold-seekers and pioneers arrived, the town quickly changed into the rough-and-ready city of San Francisco.

The city's early history is one of the great adventure stories of the American West—adventures of vigilantes and outlaws, of shanghais and secret gangs, of fortunes won and lost overnight. San Franciscans take pride in their pioneer past and work hard to save or restore historic parts of the city.

2

Gateway to Gold

For hundreds of years, European explorers sailed past a huge natural bay, midway up the coast of California. It was—and still is—one of the world's great natural harbors. The early explorers never discovered the bay's entrance because it was often hidden by heavy fogs.

The inlet to the bay—later named the Golden Gate—was finally discovered by Captain Manuel de Ayala in August 1775. One year later, an expedition made up of soldiers and Catholic priests arrived on a narrow, hilly peninsula. It overlooked the inlet to the great bay. There the soldiers built a *presidio*—a military fort—and a Catholic mission named *Misión San Francisco de Asís*. Later, a small port, and a nearby town, grew up on the peninsula in what is now downtown San Francisco. The new settlement was named *Yerba*

The Golden Gate, a strait now spanned by the Golden Gate Bridge, forms the inlet to San Francisco Bay.

Buena, the Spanish words for "good herb," after a mintlike vine that grew there.

Life in the bayside community was quiet under Spanish, and later Mexican, rule. Traders came and went. Ships visited, and then sailed on along the Pacific coast. The streets were so muddy that wagons, horses, and people often bogged down in the muck. No one paid much attention to the tiny settlement.

This peaceful period ended when war broke out between the United States and Mexico. On July 9, 1846, U.S. Navy ships sailed into the bay, and Captain John B. Montgomery raised the Stars and Stripes over the town at a place called Portsmouth Square. Yerba Buena now belonged to the United States. At the end of the Mexican War, all of California became U.S. territory.

Within a year, the Americans changed the town's name to San Francisco. It had 820 citizens, 200 houses, and one school. Then, on a May day in 1848, San Francisco's fortunes changed—from rags to riches.

Sam Brannan, a newspaper editor, ran down Montgomery Street waving a bottle full of gold dust.

"Gold!" he cried. "Gold from the American River."

Gold had been discovered in the foothills of the Sierra Nevada mountains, north and east of the city. Suddenly, San Francisco was the Golden Gate to riches. Almost 100,000 people from all over the world rushed to

Misión San Francisco de Asís, now known as Mission Dolores, marks the spot where the city was founded more than 200 years ago.

the city to seek their fortunes in the gold fields.

Some of the new arrivals stayed in San Francisco and set up businesses or found work. They supplied goods and services to the gold-seekers. Levi Strauss designed his famous work pants to stand up to the miners' rugged way of life.

People from different nations settled in separate areas that would later become San Francisco's neighborhoods. The less honest came here, too, hoping to take gold from those who had found it.

Some of the newcomers stayed only long enough to outfit themselves before leaving for the gold camps. Called the "49ers," they braved the dangers of the deserts and mountains.

Sailors abandoned their ships in the harbor to join the 49ers. To replace the lost crew members, captains used "shanghaied" men—men who were given drugged drinks in waterfront bars and then kidnapped. They awoke from their drugged sleep after they were far out to sea and could not escape.

The 49ers took more than $100 million in gold from the ground. Much of that new wealth ended up in San Francisco. After the gold strike ended, prospectors found silver in neighboring Nevada, and another boom began. Silver followed the trail of gold and poured into San Francisco. Once again, people flocked to the city in search of new fortunes.

With the arrival of money, busi-

California miners, wearing work pants made by Levi Strauss and Company.

ness, and people came crime. In fact, San Franciscans invented the word *hoodlum* to describe youth gangs. Committees of Vigilance were formed to "protect" citizens from these gangs. The committees were bands of men who took the law into their own hands. They roamed the streets and "arrested" those they believed to be criminals. Then the men "tried," "judged," and hanged the "guilty." Eventually, city leaders established law and order, and the days of the vigilantes ended.

During San Francisco's early days, people traveled around the city by horse cars and mules. One day, Andrew Hallidie, an inventor, witnessed an unusually bad horse car accident. Hallidie decided to do something about transportation in the city. That "something" was the invention of the cable car—a horseless car pulled over the hills by an underground cable.

The first cable car creaked into service on August 1, 1873. By 1890, eight cable car companies ran 600 cars over more than 100 miles (161 kilometers) of track. Since cable cars provided a safe way to travel up and down the city's steep hills, they helped make it possible for San Francisco to grow rapidly. By 1900 the city had 342,000 people.

As the nineteenth century ended, it seemed as if nothing could stop San Francisco's growth. But the good times were about to end. Just before dawn on April 18, 1906, a huge earthquake on the San Andreas Fault struck the Golden Gate city.

For almost a full minute, the earth shook as the San Andreas Fault shifted. More than 120 aftershocks—smaller earthquakes—rattled the city during that same day. Fires flared from fallen candles and chimneys. By noon, San Francisco was burning.

The fire destroyed large areas of the city in the three days following the earthquake. Fire fighters dynamited entire city blocks to create fire breaks to stop the fire. More than 500 people lost their lives.

Cable cars provide a safe way to travel up and down San Francisco's steep hills.

Market Street burning during the great earthquake of 1906.

Even this disaster didn't stop San Francisco for long. Citizens and businesses began rebuilding within days. A.P. Giannini, founder of the Bank of America, made loans to businesses from a stall on a street corner. His bank building had been destroyed in the earthquake and fire.

By 1940, the Golden Gate Bridge to the north and the San Francisco-Oakland Bay Bridge to the east connected a growing city to other parts of the Bay Area. In 1972, the opening of the computer-controlled Bay Area Rapid Transit system linked the city to the communities across the bay. Today, more than 700,000 people live in San Francisco. Several hundred thousand more commuters arrive from surrounding areas each business day.

The enormous destructive power of the earthquake left the city in ruins.

Throughout its history, from the gold rush days to modern city life, San Francisco has welcomed people from other cities and lands. The original 49ers and pioneers came to the city from many nations. Thousands of immigrants still arrive in San Francisco each year. Some join families already living here, but many arrive knowing no one and with no skills in the English language. Students begin their school life in San Francisco at Newcomer High, a special high school where they learn to read, write, and

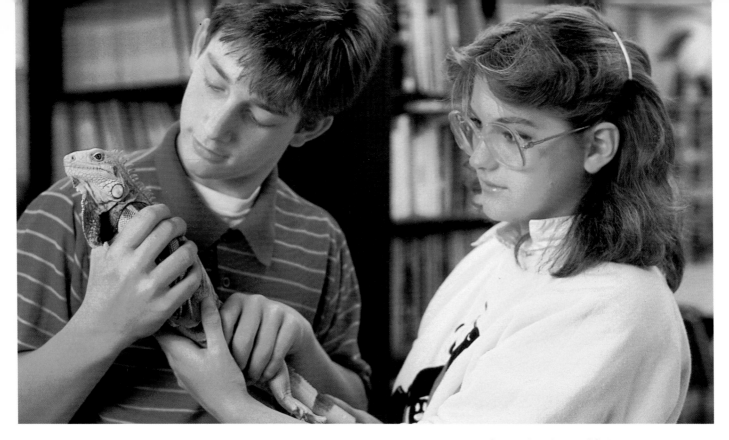

Students study nature, science, and history at classes sponsored by the California Academy of Sciences.

speak English and to understand American ways of life.

San Francisco children can also study a wide range of special subjects outside the schoolroom. Young actors and actresses attend classes offered by the American Conservatory Theatre, a highly respected acting company. The Symphony Youth Orchestra has won one of classical music's most prized awards. Ballet students keep on their toes at ballet schools, and would-be artists learn painting, sculpture, and collage at art classes throughout the city. No matter what the subject, San Francisco has a school or academy that teaches it.

Even with all it has to offer, San Francisco has problems. The need to help the homeless, the hungry, the aged, the poor, the immigrants, and many other special groups challenges city and religious leaders. Victims of the deadly disease AIDS strain the city's health care system. And yet, San Francisco survives and thrives. More and more people from just about every country on the globe call it home.

3

The Neighborhoods

Many of San Francisco's well-known neighborhoods began before the gold rush. Some neighborhoods formed around the geography of the city—"hill" neighborhoods such as Nob Hill, Russian Hill, and Telegraph Hill; valleys such as Noe Valley and Eureka Valley; and waterfront areas such as Seacliff, the Marina, and Embarcadero.

San Francisco also has neighborhoods such as Nihonmachi, Chinatown, and the Mission where people who came from particular nations live. A large homosexual, or "gay," community is centered in the Castro neighborhood. In St. Francis Wood and Pacific Heights, the city's wealthy live in one-of-a-kind mansions.

One of the oldest neighborhoods in San Francisco is Chinatown. The first Chinese arrived in San Francisco during the gold rush. Many stayed and

A view of San Francisco Bay from a "hill" neighborhood in the city.

settled near the place—Portsmouth Square—where they left their ships. Chinatown grew up around it.

The Dragon Gate on Grant Avenue forms the main entrance to Chinatown. The green tiled gate, flanked by two temple dogs, was a gift from the Republic of China (Taiwan).

Grant Avenue is lined with shops selling colorful objects and Chinese foods. Chinese jade, ivory carvings, incense sticks, dried fish, and herbs used as medicine pack store shelves and window displays. Wind chimes tinkle, and banners wave in the breeze. Smoked ducks hang in shop windows, and live squid swim in huge tanks. Along the crowded streets, Chinatown's many restaurants offer tasty foods from every district of China.

Shoppers in Chinatown.

North Beach lies next to China-town and was once a beach when part of the bay—now filled in—extended into the city. San Francisco's original Italian community settled in this area. Also called Little Italy, North Beach is known for its Italian restaurants and family-owned businesses. Here, city residents and visitors enjoy Italian sausages, fresh pasta and sauces, and cream-filled pastries.

Telegraph Hill crowns the North Beach area. In 1853, it served as the Morse Code Signal Station for ships sailing through the bay. In those days, the hill was a rounded, grassy knoll where goats grazed. Over time, sailors dug out the east side of the hill so they could use the rocks to add weight, or ballast, to their ships. Today, Tele-

Telegraph Hill rises above the city in the distance.

One of San Francisco's famous stair streets.

graph Hill's east side forms a steep cliff.

Despite modern transportation, many of the streets on Telegraph Hill can be reached only by walking up one of the city's famous stair streets. These are streets so steep that they can only be climbed by stairs built into them.

The Filbert Street Steps on Telegraph Hill wind past cottages nearly 150 years old. During the 1906 fire, residents saved the cottages by dousing them with water. If water was not available, they used red wine.

Unlike Telegraph Hill and much of the city, the Marina is a narrow belt of flat land at the northernmost tip of the San Francisco peninsula. After the 1906 earthquake and fire, San Franciscans decided to show the world that their city had risen from the ashes. They adopted the city seal and flag that showed a phoenix rising from flames. Then, they hosted the Panama-Pacific International Exposition of 1915 to celebrate the opening of the Panama Canal.

City planners turned the northern waterfront district into a wonderland. Following their plans, workers filled in more than 600 acres of bay marshland and constructed buildings to showcase exhibits and art from around the world. They also dredged up sand from the bay floor to build a seawall. After dredging, the hole left in the bottom of the bay was so deep that the planners decided to build San Francisco's Yacht Harbor there.

The exposition was a rousing success—more than 18 million visitors arrived to celebrate. One of the buildings from the exposition is the Palace of Fine Arts, home of the Exploratorium. This is a hands-on science museum where adults and children may tinker with more than 600 exhibits. Visitors have called the Exploratorium "the best science museum in the world."

Another part of San Francisco dates back to the founding of the city. A Costanoan Indian village once stood on the site of the Mission district.

Misión San Francisco de Asís was founded here in 1776.

The Mission has the best weather in the city because the hills surrounding the district hold back the fog. Often, when every other neighborhood is fog-bound, the Mission is sun-drenched.

The sunny weather caused this area to become the "fun" side of town. Gambling houses, race tracks, and amusement parks once dotted the Mission. Some of the city's finest homes were built here, and many still stand.

The Mission, the Marina, North Beach, and Chinatown cover just some of San Francisco's many neighborhoods. Nearly 100 neighborhood associations exist to protect each area and to create the best future for the people who live there. San Franciscans take pride in their international blend of customs and ways of life and work hard to preserve them.

Young people explore the "Silage Beach" exhibit at the Exploratorium.

4

San Francisco—Just for Fun

People of all ages find places to have fun in San Francisco. The city has much to offer—museums, theaters, and parks, as well as beautiful places where young and old can sail, fish, and run. In fact, San Francisco has been called "America's Favorite City" because of its many attractions.

Visitors and residents enjoy the city's parks—120 parks of all sizes. No matter where they go, a nearby patch of green stands out among the concrete of the city. Children can play in more than seventy playgrounds and swim in ten pools. The city has more than five miles (eight kilometers) of ocean beach, a fishing pier, a yacht harbor, and many tennis courts.

However, no place offers quite as much as the 1,017 acres (412 hectares) of Golden Gate Park. On warm days, on foggy days, on cold rainy days,

Sailboats line the beach in the Golden Gate National Recreation Area.

people go to Golden Gate Park. If the weather does not allow visitors to have a picnic, hike the trails, or toss a Frisbee, they may go to one of the museums or watch the dolphins being fed at Steinhart Aquarium.

At the aquarium, visitors can view—and sometimes touch—some of the 14,000 aquatic animals housed there, including penguins, dolphins, seals, and crocodiles. The aquarium forms one part of the world-famous California Academy of Sciences. The academy also houses Morrison Planetarium and Laserium as well as a natural history museum.

A century ago, experts said Golden Gate Park could never be built. The site for the park, called the Outside Lands, was so sandy and so windy that everything planted there blew away. Still, since the land was cheap and available, city leaders set it aside for the park.

In the 1870s, John McLaren, a young Scottish landscape gardener, took up the task of building the park. He arranged with the city to have wagon load after wagon load of horse manure carted to the site. The young Scot used the manure to build a layer of soil on the sandy ground. Then, he anchored the soil and sand with special grasses and shrubs. He shoveled the sand away from his plantings day after day after day until the plants were big enough to hold their own.

McLaren wanted to make the park a "window into nature," and he worked the rest of his life to achieve

Young people learn about the planets and stars at Morrison Planetarium.

that goal. When he was eighty, he planted redwood trees as a gift to future generations of park visitors. Fifty years later, McLaren's redwood trees were thirty feet (nine meters) high.

Today, when visitors to Golden Gate Park see its beautiful plants, flowers, waterfalls, ponds, lakes, and meadows, they know that McLaren succeeded in making the park a window into nature. Golden Gate Park is a work of living art.

Yet the park is more than plants

and trees. Summer music concerts fill the air at the bandshell across from the Academy of Sciences. The M. H. de Young Memorial Museum and Asian Art Museum display art and artifacts (objects) from around the world and from every historical age.

San Francisco's first zoo opened in 1856 in a downtown basement. Its main attractions were chained bears.

Today's zoo, now located south of Golden Gate Park at Ocean Beach, opened in 1889. It has no chains, and very few barred cages. More than 1,000 animals from around the world live in cleverly designed, barless display areas. Visitors may see koalas, polar bears, a snow leopard, and Prince Charles, a rare white tiger. Wolves roam in their own specially

Left: The Japanese Tea Garden at Golden Gate Park. *Right*: Prince Charles, the white tiger at the San Francisco Zoo.

Cooking fresh seafood at Fisherman's Wharf.

built homes. Monkeys and apes romp in the Primate Discovery Center, known worldwide for its excellent design.

The zoo is near the Pacific Ocean on the city's southwest side. Since San Francisco is a waterfront city, some of its most interesting places lie where the city meets the ocean and the bay. The city's fishermen dock their boats at Fisherman's Wharf. While the fleet is much smaller than it once was, it still brings about 21 million pounds (9.5 million kilograms) of fish into San Francisco each year. In addition to fresh rock cod, sole, salmon, and herring, people can buy fresh crab and shrimp cocktails from street vendors who cook shellfish in huge metal kettles right on the sidewalk.

Boats from San Francisco's fishing fleet dock at Fisherman's Wharf.

The Golden Gate National Recreation Area covers a large part of San Francisco's waterfront on the ocean and bay sides. This public wilderness area also includes parts of Marin County to the north. Within it are historic sites, museums, beaches, and the headquarters of the U.S. Sixth Army. The army headquarters, called the *Presidio*, served as the Spanish army post more than two centuries ago.

Today, Alcatraz Island in San Francisco Bay forms one part of the Golden Gate National Recreation Area. From 1934 to 1963, Alcatraz, nicknamed the Rock, served as an "escape-proof" federal prison. Dangerous currents and cold waters surrounding the island made it difficult to escape from Alcatraz. Now the empty

cell blocks of this famous prison are open to visitors from around the world.

San Francisco's waterfront serves as the start and finish for its most well known race. The Bay to Breakers foot race in May is a rugged, 6.73-mile (10.84-kilometer) run from the bay to the ocean, up and over the long, tough Hayes Street hill.

Serious runners come from around the world to compete in the Bay to Breakers. Others, who are not trying to win, also take part and turn the middle part of the race into a fun run. Costumed runners dressed like centipedes, pieces of fruit, and giant running shoes jog along the course behind the more serious runners. They help make this race another reason

Alcatraz Island, and the famous former prison, in San Francisco Bay.

that San Franciscans and visitors enjoy the city by the bay.

Mention San Francisco to people who have visited the city, and they think of its breathtaking hilltop views, its colorful international population, and its fabulous food. San Francisco is known for many things—the natural beauty of its bayside location, the music, art, and recreation throughout the city, the mild climate, and the great variety of things to see and do. For all these reasons, San Francisco truly is "America's Favorite City."

The San Francisco-Oakland Bay Bridge and the city shine brightly at night.

Places to Visit in San Francisco

Performing Arts

American Conservatory Theatre (ACT)
415 Geary Street
(415) 673-6440
Nationally known acting company that offers classes for young actors/actresses

San Francisco Ballet
Opera House
Van Ness Avenue and Grove Street
(415) 621-3838

San Francisco Opera
Opera House
Van Ness Avenue and Grove Street
(415) 864-3330

San Francisco Symphony
Davies Symphony Hall
Van Ness Avenue and Grove Street
(415) 431-5400

Art Museums

Asian Art Museum
Golden Gate Park
(415) 668-8921

California Palace of the Legion of Honor
Lincoln Park
(415) 750-3600

Chinese Culture Center
750 Kearny Street
Third floor of the Holiday Inn
(415) 986-1822

M.H. de Young Memorial Museum
Golden Gate Park
(415) 750-3600

Mexican Museum of San Francisco
Fort Mason Center, Building D
Laguna and Marina Boulevard
(415) 441-0404

Museo Italo Americano
Fort Mason Center, Building C
Laguna and Marina Boulevard
(415) 673-2200

San Francisco Museum of Modern Art
War Memorial Veterans Building
Van Ness Avenue and McAllister Street
(415) 863-8800

Science Museums

California Academy of Sciences
Golden Gate Park
(415) 221-5100

Exploratorium
Palace of Fine Arts
3601 Lyon Street at Marina Boulevard
(415) 563-3200

Randall Junior Museum
199 Museum Way
(415) 863-1399
Science museum for children and adults

Historical Museums

Cable Car Museum
Washington and Mason streets
(415) 474-1887

Fort Point National Historic Site
Presidio of San Francisco
(415) 556-2857

Mission Dolores
16th and Dolores
(415) 621-8203

National Maritime Museum
Aquatic Park at foot of Polk Street
(415) 556-8177

San Francisco African-American Historical
and Cultural Society
Fort Mason Center
Building C
Marina Boulevard and Laguna
(415) 441-0640

San Francisco History Room and Archives
Larkin and McAllister streets
(415) 558-3949
Third floor of the public library

SS Jeremiah O'Brien
Fort Mason Center
Pier 3 East
Marina Boulevard and Laguna
(415) 441-3101
The last working Liberty Ship from World War II

Wells Fargo History Room
Wells Fargo Bank
420 Montgomery Street
(415) 396-2619

Special Places

Alcatraz Island
San Francisco Bay
Contact Golden Gate National Recreation Area

Angel Island
San Francisco Bay
Department of Parks and Recreation
Marin District
1455-A E. San Francisco Boulevard
San Rafael, CA 94901
(415) 435-3522
Ellis Island of the West

Candlestick Park
San Francisco, CA 94124
(415) 468-3700
    Giants: (415) 467-8000
    49ers: (415) 468-2249

Golden Gate National Recreation Area
National Park Service
Upper Fort Mason
(415) 556-0560

Golden Gate Park
McLaren Lodge
Fell and Stanyon streets
(415) 558-3706

San Francisco Zoo
Sloat Boulevard at Pacific Ocean
(415) 661-4844

Additional information can be obtained from these agencies:

San Francisco Chamber of Commerce
465 California Street
San Francisco, CA 94101
(415) 387-5052

San Francisco Convention and Visitors Bureau
Hallidie Plaza, Powell and Market streets
San Francisco, CA 94102
(415) 974-6900

San Francisco: A Historical Time Line

1769	San Francisco Bay is discovered
1775	Alcatraz Island is discovered
1776	*Misión San Francisco de Asís* is founded
1846	American flag is raised in Portsmouth Square
1848	Gold is discovered in the Sierra Nevada foothills
1854	The first Bay Area lighthouse is built on Alcatraz Island
1869	The transcontinental railroad is completed
1870	The city begins building Golden Gate Park
1871	The San Francisco Art Institute—the first art school on the West Coast—opens
1873	The first cable car begins running
1876	Electricity lights up the city for the first time
1896	The Ferry building opens
1904	A. P. Giannini opens the Bank of Italy, which will become the Bank of America
1906	Earthquake and fire destroy the city
1915	Panama-Pacific Exposition is held; the current city hall is built
1927	San Francisco International Airport opens
1934	Alcatraz Island becomes a federal prison; Coit Tower is built
1936	The San Francisco-Oakland Bay Bridge opens
1937	The Golden Gate Bridge opens
1939	Treasure Island is built for the Golden Gate International Exposition
1945	Delegates from fifty nations meet in the city and sign the United Nations Charter
1960	The sports arena, Candlestick Park, opens

1963   Alcatraz Island prison closes; prisoners transferred to more modern federal prisons

1972   Bay Area Rapid Transit (BART) begins service between San Francisco and other Bay Area communities; the Transamerica Pyramid opens

1978   Mayor George Moscone and city supervisor Harvey Milk are killed by city supervisor Dan White

1988   The huge quilt made by the NAMES Project is displayed in twenty-five U.S. cities. Each of the nearly 2,000 pieces of the quilt is dedicated to an AIDS victim

Index